Christoph T. M. Krause

Tina – My Best Friend

My Bitch from Sri Lanka

Christoph T. M. Krause

TINA

~

My Best Friend

My Bitch from Sri Lanka

© 2020 Christoph T. M. Krause
Cover Design, Illustration: Christoph T. M. Krause
Christoph T. M. Krause, Heerstr. 394a, EU-D-Berlin.
Translation from German by Angelika Hinchcliffe, UK.
Publisher and Print: tredition GmbH,
Halenreie 42, D-22359 Hamburg

978-3-347-17257-9 (Paperback)
978-3-347-17258-6 (Hardcover)
978-3-347-17259-3 (e-Book)

Bibliographic information from the German National Library:
The German National Library lists this publication in the
German National Bibliography; detailed bibliographical data
are available via Internet at http://dnb.d-nb.de.

C O N T E N T

This book is dedicated to Tina, Mickey, Beauty und Roxy

~ Preface ~

1990 was a positive and fateful year for Germany.

The world around Germany changed as well. New states were founded, others were dissolved and revolutions bore their fruit.

For me, it was a year that changed everything in my life. I went on an adventure trip to Sri Lanka and found my love for a dog.

From this point on, my life changed drastically and turned into something completely different. However, it also introduced certain dark elements. A life-threatening disease was only one of several strokes of fate.

All these changes started with a small dog, who I brought home from Ceylon.

8 years later I turned my passion for dogs into a job, which I still carry out successfully to this day.

All that was possible because of what happened one day in March of 1990 in Kandy, Sri Lanka.

In this book, I finally get to tell this very personal story.

~ Holiday at Last ~

For many years I took exotic trips to Sri Lanka.

As soon as you get off the plane and arrive on the runway via the gangway, you are overwhelmed by the humid climate of this beautiful fairyland called Ceylon.

Mystic and exotic like India, Sri Lanka, which is how it was named in 1972, is reminiscent of a drop located on the south coast of India. It is only about five degrees of latitude away from the equator.

In practical terms, this means that the seasons are not at all comparable to what they are like in Europe. There are only monsoon seasons that bring a lot of rain and non-monsoon seasons during which there are droughts, even though they are moist and humid.

"Rain" during monsoon season means, that the rain pours down from the sky like rivers, flooding everything that was not prepared for it.

Due to the sewage systems in towns and villages being broken most of the time and neither receiving maintenance nor repairs, ever since the British installed them, they can't collect large quantities of water. This results in pedestrians often having to wade through knee-deep water in order to cross any regular road.

A region without any seasons means that you get to experience something fundamentally different than what the average Central European is used to.

We grew up with the temperatures as well as the brightness of the day changing constantly. In summer it gets light early and it gets dark late and it winter the opposite happens.

We require heating, in order to protect ourselves from the cold in our homes and we have known since we were children, that it is necessary to adapt our clothing to the temperature.

This experience almost seems to be "God-given" and irrefutable; ask yourself if you have ever wondered, whether this could be different, before you went to such countries.

Of course you know it and so do I. I've known it since Geography class in school. But experiencing it is an entirely different story.

Now you travel to Asia and wonder why the pavements get "folded up" at 6 pm in the evening (provided there are any!).

You wonder, why it gets light at 6 am and dark at 6 pm all year round, without any noticeable change or shift in the course of the year!

It was a cultural shock for me.

I once spent the night of Christmas Eve in a hotel pool right by the Indian ocean. It was about 30 degrees and in the background you could hear the song "Holy Night" in German. I have to say I truly felt as if I was in a film and a wrong one at that.

The temperature is essentially always the same, always around 30 degrees Celsius, all year long.

A Central European is not made for such conditions, even if he believes in it at first or longs for it in his dreams.

I, for one, found out that these experiences made me appreciate the different seasons. I enjoy them because they correspond with my nature.

Of course we don't like the cold and wet days in autumn and winter at first, but as soon as we have experienced the opposite, even once in our lives, we start to think and feel differently.

However, that is something that everyone has to experience themselves.

I'm certain that there are people who deal well with it and therefore love it.

~ The First Cultural Shock ~

Heat and humidity take hold of the newcomer as soon as the doors of the airplane are opened and at first you have a hard time imagining how you are supposed to endure that for the entire duration of your time there.

The airport was already considered quite modern and internationally designed in the 1980s.

After your first step out of the airport, you are once again stoked at the dimensions.

Hundreds of people are waiting in front of the building, curiously watching the newcomers, anticipating business connections or other contacts. Taxi drivers in particular are waiting right here for new customers. Even if they only have „tuk tuks"[1] to offer or sometimes donkey carriages to take tourists to their destinations.

As I mostly travel privately and not on a package deal, there was no tourist bus ready to pick me up. As an experienced traveller to Ceylon, I organised my own personal driver, who was waiting for me patiently.

---

[1] A car rickshaw is a motorised version of a Rikscha, which has its origins in Japan. These are small vehicles with two or three wheels that are either pulled by a person on foot or on a bicycle (cycle rickshaw) and are used for transporting goods or persons. Due to the noise that the two-stroke engine typically makes, there are sometimes called tuk tuk.

Internet quoting: URL. https://de.wikipedia.org/wiki/Autorikscha.html.
Status: Oct. 17th, 2020. Translated from German by Angelika Hinchcliffe. UK.

~ We are Heroes ~

I quickly walked past all those that were waiting, but not without having my light-coloured skin touched as I brushed past them, as some considered it "God-like". It was apparently a new sight for many Ceylonese people and lead to some joyful reactions.

Us Europeans (as well as other people) love to tan our mostly pale skin in summer by means of sun bathing (and perhaps even the use of tanning beds). We do that in order to reach a more desirable "brown" colour, which suggests that we may also participate in the nimbus of a fit, modern human, but sadly only for a short period of time.

It seems as though the behaviour of the locals is the exact opposite. The lighter the skin is and the more blond your hair is, the more desirable. Quite a few locals dye their hair blonde or a different light colour in order to conform to this concept.

I have always found this strange twisting of these ideal images to be quite bizarre. Even though it shows that humans tend to never be satisfied with what we are and what we have. Instead we always look at our neighbour's "happiness" and try to imitate him or her.

The "hero worship", given to our species, has always seemed very submissive to me, even though I never felt uncomfortable being touched. Their touches never felt demanding or presumptuous, but shy and full of respect for, what the locals considered "God-like", ideal images.

I have to say that this "cult of worship" made me feel alienated to a great extent. Especially since I knew about the colonial history of the British, the Dutch and the Portuguese, who had not treated the locals delicately, to say the least. Bizarrely, this is what made it come full circle in my mind.

Colonialism was only possible, because lots of Asians traditionally seemed to exhibit a "natural" reverence for Europeans, at least during colonial times, which might have been why the European's behaviour during those times was tolerated by them.

Of course, this also says something about how this people or rather this ethnic group sees itself. Do they consider themselves equal, do they have feelings of inferiority, wherever those come from? Or are these feelings of inferiority a sort of tradition, or maybe it is just our impression? Is it perhaps a question of politeness and respect towards strangers and has nothing to do with subservience?

Should we even generalise these impressions or does it require an empirical investigation?

These questions need to be answered by scientists. This experience was very new to me. But I do understand the temptation it holds.

I once was invited to the home of a Ceylonese middle class family. The conditions were very similar to European palaces, expect that it was a small townhouse.

Being their guest, I was provided with all-round care by their staff. Without ever having to ask for it, my shoes were polished, my suitcase was unpacked and everything was arranged in a way that made me feel like a king who did the family's bidding.

My overnight accommodation was with the youngest son, who was 13 years old. We shared a double bed.

This decision seemed the strangest to me, as I was not sure whether this meant that they offered their own son as a present to me (I heard that those things really do happen).

On the other hand, it could have also meant, that the parents trusted me a great deal and wanted to show me their respect.

I am sure that the parents knew I wouldn't abuse this situation, but how can you be really sure of that? Nowadays we know what kind of things go on in the world, but back then you didn't talk about those things, especially in Sri Lanka. It seemed as though there was no other place to stay in the house.

All these seemingly contradicting experiences were pivotal and I felt like I was on a volcano. I always felt as if the house of cards inside of me could collapse at any moment. The experiences I had in this country, regardless of their nature, were disconcerting and enticing at the same time.

Who wouldn't like to have their own personal staff for only a small price and have them care for you all day, every day?

My answer is: yes and no. Culturally it is very strange and tempting all at once. It is precisely this ambivalence that makes this country what it is. It is equally shocking and fascinating.

"Heaven and hell" all in one. A catapult of positive emotions and horror scenarios. Asia at its best.

Over the centuries, many people have succumbed to these experiences in their colonies. They were absorbed by the diversity, the sweet temptations and the worst horrors imaginable. Poverty and misery are just around the corner. It is right next to all the colonial glitz and glamour that I experienced.

Huge slums in the towns, hundreds of thousands of people, who have to live in street gutters. There is sickness and death and it all happened just around the corner.

Back to the behaviour of the locals and the traditional admiration they have for Europeans.

It has certainly changed fundamentally after all these years, especially because of the increase in experiences that people make through mass tourism.

Their behaviour towards tourists has apparently always been motivated by the fact that lots of locals thought, that if they had good connections to tourists, they could make it to Europe. Then they could profit from the flowing "milk and honey" and all the money lying on the streets, without having to work too much.

This might sound stuck-up, arrogant or racist, but it is not. I got to know the country and its inhabitants over many years and I had lots of conversations, I invited locals to Europe and more.

Even their own experiences in Europe, even as tourists, have not altered the basic behaviour and the inner attitude of many locals from Sri Lanka. If anything, it was strengthened. I would cautiously call it "cultural discrepancy".

To sum it up briefly:

Many locals from Sri Lanka (and probably many other nationalities in Africa and Asia) seem to admire Europe or the "Western world" (we can also see it in the current refugee crisis).

They obviously thought that all Europeans were rich. Who else could afford to go on holiday on the white sand beaches of Ceylon, unless they are Croesus?

It seemed as though you could find money on the streets in Europe. Even members of the government offered homes and other benefits to immigrants and refugees.

Even if one didn't realise that you have to work in Europe too and that life is not super easy and convenient for everybody. These well intentioned warnings were immediately dismissed, these people didn't believe they were true. It just couldn't be!

Those people who originally come from near the equator could not imagine the cold, bad weather. Just like I couldn't imagine what it would be like to live near the equator, before I (like I described earlier) experienced it first hand.

It makes sense that anyone who was unemployed and didn't have a lot of money (there were and are lots of people) tried with all their might to get to the place where they imagined flowing milk and honey.

I have to admit, I would want and do the same thing.

~ A Trip to Wonderland ~

As soon as you enter the country from the airport, you have to know that even in our view, short distances lead to unusually long travel times. For example, 20 KM from the airport to Negombo takes one hour, sometimes even one and a half. Bad roads, no feeder roads or motorways, lots of traffic from all directions, such as donkey carts, pedestrians walking in all directions, cows on the road, tuk-tuks, motorbikes, bicycles, etc. blocked the streets in a way that you could only drive at the same speed as you would walk.

Apart from the horrible stench of terrible exhaust fumes, whirled up dirt and dust, constant honking, and so on, this journey made you feel like you were on a psychedelic trip.

If you agree to such a horror drive you suddenly become part of this madness and you think it is intoxicating.

The impressions of this first trip, no matter its destination, leave newcomers wanting for more. He or she dives into a wonderful adventure world of different sensations.

After a half hour ride the European tourist is so exhausted by all these impressions, smells, acoustic waterfalls and chaotic streets that he arrives at his destination tired when the only thing left to do, after a long flight and a crazy trip to his or her personal destination, is to sink into his mattress completely worn out and in desperate need for sleep.

When you arrive here in the jungle of Sri Lankas, even though it is still quite close to the coast, you first have to acclimatise to the area for a few days. It is best to do this at the beach. It helps to go for a swim in the Indian Ocean, which has a temperature of over 30 degrees. Even when it rains it feels warmer in the water than outside.

A sunrise or sunset on the beach is more relaxing than anything else. They are often very colourful and put you in a kind of trance, as you sit on the beach and all there is left to do is marvel.

Within the first few days of your stay it is particularly nice when you are approached by (local) pedlars on the beach, who have all sorts of (mostly useless) stuff to offer. However, it is still better than having children offer their bodies, which unfortunately, happens very often in these countries.

It doesn't happen as obviously, sometimes you don't realise it right away. But if you listen (and look) closely, the behaviour of some children and teenagers is very obvious. Of course they have made experience with this and go about it with extreme caution and reservation. They naturally exhibit "helpful" signals, which often leads to something that should never happen. You could observe that adult males, seemingly from Europe, went on walks with little boys and girls.

As soon as you, a European, have put on some colour, which happens in only a few days, as the skin tans (often also reddens) fairly quickly, people will stop approaching you. That is when the locals realise that this tourist knows a bit more now and can't be addressed as easily, or is no longer willing to buy anything useless.

At one point I spent my whole day lying under a beach umbrella on the beach that was near my hotel and reading my book. The sky was cloudy all day long and no one would have seen any danger in this behaviour, which was deemed cautious by Europeans.

The rays of the sun are felt so intensely near the equator, that sitting in the shade of a beach umbrella won't even change anything about the fact that you fall prey to a relentless sunburn after only a few hours, sometimes even just half an hour. This is what happened to me and it took more than a week for this incredible pain to subside.

When it comes to „Beach People", you have to imagine the following:

In the 80s a local who "had made it" and worked in a hotel as a waiter or room service assistant earned about 30 Euros per day (converted).

That was about the same as the cost of one night in a hotel room which was booked privately, as opposed to as part of a deal.

An unskilled worker who worked at a construction site, for example, would have only earned 0.25 Euros per day.

Now it is a bit easier to understand why tourists are seen as a sort of "victim", who can help you fill your pockets with plenty of money in a matter of minutes.

"Does it still make sense to work on construction sites?", many might ask.

Another example is a teenager who sells his body for 20 Euros. After making this experience once he will never go back to his regular work. It is a lot more lucrative to serve tourists.

This is a crux in tourism all around the world. In many cases, tourism destroys social and societal constructs and leads to locals depending on visitors to an extreme degree and in every area.

At the same time tourism yields lots of money, at least in official, legal sectors and can lead to prosperity and even wealth.

That is if we ignore the illegal "black market of sex tourism" and similar dubious businesses like the sale and enslavement of children.

This dependence of countries like Sri Lanka and many others like it, which are also reliant on tourism as their only source of income results in a strong social and economical imbalance. As soon as there is a crisis of any kind, which causes the tourism to die down, i.e. civil war, conflicts or a pandemic, the fatal consequences of this one sided dependence come to light.

After a few days of acclimatizing physically as well as psychologically, it is time to take small trips and excursions to the heartland or the beautiful coastlines.

The beaches on the south coast are very interesting. It is easy to get there by train, which takes its route right along the west coast, providing a fantastic view of the ocean.

In this area you can live right under the palm trees at the beach in cabanas[2]. It is such a unique beach by the South sea and is most often empty, which leaves you to marvel.

In the surroundings of the cabanas you can usually see

hard working helpers (cabana boys) whose job it is to keep the beach nice and tidy by sweeping the sand, serving drinks and preparing meals, often all day long right on the open fire.

---

[2] Originally, the word "cabana", is Spanish and can be translated by hut or little house. Sometimes the expression is used for changing rooms at the beach site or at pools in hotels.

The employees often live there as well, which just means that they camp in a hammock or underneath a table somewhere in the area. This way they also fulfil the role of security guard, watching everything on the property 24/7.

Whoever has made this kind of experience once in their lives, will never forget the feeling of bliss and harmony, provided that he or she doesn't have a bad conscience because he or she has succumbed to the genuine temptations of the tropics.

~ Fruit Market in Kandy ~

The taxi is hot. Our drive through the highlands of this wonderful country has its challenges. The roads are tricky, it is humid and the traffic is dreadful. Oxcarts, bicycles, animals of all kinds, loads of people, motor vehicles of all kinds clog up the hot country roads on the way to the highlands and turn our trip into the ultimate adventure.

I feel as though I am on a fantasy journey. Every kilometre that we cover in our 30 year old Morris seems so strange, I feel carried away. The car lacks a tread pattern and the petrol can is located by the feet of the passenger seat. A small hose leads to the engine compartment and feeds the ancient motor with the expensive liquid.

Every two seconds someone honks their horn; it would be impossible to navigate the road network of this country without a horn.

After several hours of this madness we finally arrive at our destination Kandy, located in the highlands of Sri Lanka. A town that is at a high altitude, but it still feels as warm as the lower parts of the island. If you go a bit higher up into the mountains it can get quite cold at night.

Kandy (in Sinhala[3]: Maha Nuvara = big city) is an old Sinhala royal city. It was conquered by the British in 1815, after a long struggle and from then on it was modernised by the British. In 1867 it was connected to the railway line from Colombo.

In the centre of town, there is a large "tank", the „Kandy Lake". These tanks consist of water reservoirs that the British constructed. In German you would call them "artificial lakes". The tanks have a rectangular or square shape.

Next to the tank, there is a large, significant tooth temple called Sri Dalada Maligawa. Legend has it, that it houses one of Buddha's teeth. This is the reason why lots of Buddhist pilgrims travel to this temple once a year. They come to town to celebrate this treasure with colourful and loud processions.

A visit to a famous fruit market was also part of our plan. Our taxi driver told us about an interesting sight, which was almost too much to handle after such an exhausting journey through the dream world of Sri Lanka.

---

[3] Also called **Sinhalese** or **Singhalese**

In the centre of the picture you can recognize the atrium's areal of the fruit market.

My friend Manuel stayed in the car. He is quite young and only cares about certain "youth topics". Fruit and meat markets are not part of that.

Defiant and convinced that he wouldn't miss the slightest thing, he puts on his walkman and leans back on the old, tattered grey plastic seats of our car. Then he dreams of our destination for the day, a pool and… he has already fallen asleep.

Main entrance of the fruit market.

The fruit market is more of an inner-city meeting spot of this old royal mountain town Kandy, than what it actually should be.

Everything in Kandy is influenced, built or organised by the British in some way. They were the last colonial power of Ceylon. It is possible to still recognised the European structures of this market in all their glory. Asians would have probably not built stone houses in the atrium style, in order to sell spices, fruit and meat there.

They put sheds by the roadside, built stands out of boards using an ancient cloth as protection from the sun. But they wouldn't build stone houses with roofs!

At least such platitudes keep haunting our clueless thoughts.

I can still recognise the splendour of yesteryear, which has long since made way for an unbelievable patina. A patina that we don't even come close to seeing anywhere in Europe.

The plaster on the walls is probably one hundred years old. If not, it would still look the same, since the moist tropical air treats everything the same, no matter how recently it was built or how old it might be.

The colours on the walls were never updated or painted again. The roofs have become rotten and they are leaking, so that the monsoon rain flows through every crack of every market stand and covers everything that is not protected by some dirty plastic tarpaulin or coconut leaves.

Hundreds of people are pushing their way through the atrium area whilst lamenting loudly. They hurry from one stand to the next, haggling, trading, shouting, crying or laughing.

What sounds like a Babylonian jumble of languages, including Sinhalese, Tamils, Arabs, Europeans and a few Americans enters my ear, mixed in with the voices of our small travel group, which alternate making excited and shocked sounds. It all depends on the variety of colours and shapes of the fruit or the state of the market.

Bunches of flies surround every piece of meat. Meat, that is dangling down from poles or hooks on dirty ancient roof gables and waiting to be put in the wood- or coal-fired cooking pot of a large family soon enough.

Our group stops at the stand with bananas in all kinds of colours and sizes. These tropical fruits are shining brightly from a glittering hook, waiting to be bought by the mother of a large family and maybe getting eaten by dozens of hungry mouths.

~ Tina ~

The centre of the atrium is just grass.

A whole pile of rubbish was dumped there. The shop-keepers use this patch of grass for one reason only: as a waste area. Nobody cares about what it looks like.

The beauty of the ancient Asian culture vanishes in the dirt and the industrial waste of this "threshold nation"-society (the politically incorrect term used to be: Third World).

Rats run through the scenery, as if it was the most ordinary thing in the world. Crows release deafening screeches and attack anything that looks edible.

It is like falling into a trance, when you surrender to this setting; a trance within a dream world of smells, sounds and heat, combined with breathtaking beauty and dizzying ugliness, paired with ancient rituals and seasoned with modern accessories.

In the middle of this apocalypse of "A thousand and one nights" I discover a being, that seems to play around undisturbed with a much too large bone, with pleasure and full focus. As if it was the first, the most beautiful and the last bone in its life.

I feel as though I was struck by lightning. Something pulls me as if with magic, something draws me under a spell, without me knowing what is happening to me.

Before I know it, I have left the big crowd and head towards the graceful creature in the centre of the grass area, in the middle of all the chaos of this market, this town, this country.

This moment becomes the centre of my thoughts and most importantly of my emotions. Time seems to stand still.

It is a moment of karma that grips you. You know it, but you don't. This is the moment when everything in your life changes, when it is determined who you are, will be or always were.

It is the moment of "Kismet", of fate, of destiny that calls me. It calls, no, it whispers quietly; it pulls me like a magnet, stronger than anything else in my life before.

Yes, there you are, you little creature without a name, without time and space. You being of the highest spheres, **Tina, my best friend**, my first big canine love.

Is she just a dog? A puppy? I know that she is far more than that, she has already become my whole life.

~ Tina, my Best Friend ~

"Take her with you!", I can hear a voice behind me. I carry the tiny dog in my arms, she is dirty and maybe even sick. I can see that right away, but she is okay (I quickly notice she is a female). She's looking at me with her brown doe eyes, as if she wanted to say, yes, take me with you, I need you, I need your love and closeness. I am on my own. I am a stray without a choice, I don't have a mother or father anymore. My siblings are gone, I am all alone!

My mind says, I can't do that. I can't take a dog from Sri Lanka with me! Surely she has to be quarantined, she is sick, I can't take her on the plane. What will my friends think? What am I doing here?!

Before I realise it, I am on my way to the taxi, I am leaving the market, leaving the chaos, I want to get out of here. Maybe someone will come and take her from me, maybe she belongs to someone? What am I doing here?

"You are crazy", some of my companions tell me when I take the dog to the car. "He just wants to show it to Manuel" the others say. "I'm sure he will think about it." "Anything is possible when it comes to him." "He has always been a bit crazy!"

I asked the meat vendor who gave me the dog to sell me a piece of meat. I purchased 3 kilograms of raw meat. I thought I had to give her something to eat.

My taxi driver promises to cook it for me at his home; seeing as we are just passing through, we live in hotels and inns. You can't cook in there. A short while later, when we spent the night with Tina somewhere in the jungle, I was woken by a very unpleasant smell. It turned out to be the meat, which had spoiled within a few hours of not being chilled, due to the tropical heat.

I had no choice but to fling it out the window and into the jungle that surrounded the house.

In the end the only thing we could do was to buy Corned Beef in cans, as there was no way of acquiring anything else suitable or something simple such as dog food on our trip.

Luckily, Tina liked eating this meat. This is how we provided her with food while we were travelling.

Manuel patiently listens to what I have to say. He's still sitting in the taxi and listening to music; he thinks she is adorable and gives her a name: "**Tina, my best friend**", he says.

Initially I wanted to call her Kandy, because she is from Kandy and Candy means sweet in English. It would have worked well, too!

Manuel hears this phrase through his headphones: "Tina, my best friend" by Andrea Jürgens (a German child singer in the 1970s and in my opinion, this song and the singer were terrible!) and that's it.

Manuel has the word. He is young and can easily influence the situation, he is influencing me. I respect this moment and I give in.

Yes, it's **Tina** that I am holding in my arms like a newborn baby, as if she had just seen the light of the world for the first time, the light of my world.

She has always been this "light!, this Tina.

I think it was the best decision in her life to be named this way, because she is my Tina, like from a picture book and she is my best friend.

This name was a lucky choice. A gut decision, a charismatic, karmic gut decision, maybe even prophesy?

~ Royal Botanical Garden ~

Our next destination is another relic of the British colonial period; a beautifully designed tropical park, covering 80-hectares. It is called "Royal Botanical Garden" Peradeniya.

This park is hundreds of years old[4] and showcases bamboo forests as tall as houses, some trees as large and extensive as an entire forest.

A colourful display of exotic flowers makes us forget that we are still in the centre of this Asian chaos.

The park gives the impression as if time stood still, as if the English governor was still in charge. This oasis is perfect for taking a break from stressful everyday life in a modern Asian industrial society.

On the meadows you can see thousands of Sinhalese and Tamils with large groups of children, sitting or lying and eating their packed meals, mostly Rice and Curry, a national dish with rice as the base and lots of small side dishes like fish, meat and vegetables. They proudly

---

[4] See Internet quoting: URL
https://en.wikipedia.org/wiki/Royal_Botanical_Gardens,_Peradeniya.
Wikipedia: Keyword „Royal botanical garden Peradeniya", Status: Oct 26th, 2020.

wrapped them in newspaper sheets and are now eating them together with the others.

With kid and caboodle, generations of locals participate in this social game. Everyone eats using their hands and in a way that seems to us Europeans like a relic left over from a distant past.

The fingers on the right, clean hand are used to dig into the food like a shovel, turn it slightly and pick up a considerable amount of the spicy dish. Then the thumb, being used as a spoon-fork-knife-hybrid, enters the mouth in a way that allows the steaming delicacy to quickly disappear in the mouth. Soon after the hand returns to the mixture of rice and various other ingredients, all which are seasoned with lots of spices. Us Europeans would think we will never be able to taste anything else again.

In this hundredfold ceremony, which seems like a simultaneous interconnection of up and down movements of the hands, like a symphony of arms and mouths, in front of this natural backdrop which was the garden, you can hear people laughing, see them gesturing and talking. It is a delight to just observe.

Large school groups gathered together in the shade of a tropical tree to eat lunch. Despite the shade, we have to endure a heavy heat and humidity. The air causes us to be lethargic and apathetic…

Even the nearby broad river Mahaweli, that bubbles through the garden doesn't provide the desired air circulation, that we expected from a river such as this one.

A risky wooden suspension bridge spans the river, hanging freely. To the horror of someone who has a fear of heights like me, you could see the bridge swinging back and forth. Here and there it offers a good view of the bottom of the river, which continues to move untamed and foaming.

The countless wooden planks of the bridge are either broken or missing entirely. Crossing this bride becomes an adventure of itself, just like everything else here in Asia.

We decided to take a different path, past a trellis of palm trees, as tall as houses and lining the left and right of the road.

Tina runs along with us, as if she has always been our dog. She already responds to her new name, even after a few hours. It's strange, because she just joined our group a little while ago, however, it seems as if it had always been like this. Her almost bare little tail with a white tip dances funnily to the beat of her clumsy style of walking. Her fox-brown fur, still very tousled and dirty, covered with lice and ticks, gives me an idea of how pretty it could one day be. If only we had the means to care for it here.

My thoughts are circling around this problem. I ask Premadasa, our taxi driver, who always has a piece of advice at the ready; he already figured out where we can buy anti-parasite-powder. He says it is like a magic cure against anything creeping and crawling.

I need to be patient for only a little while longer, because first we want to explore the park some more, discover its beauty, enjoy its shade and rejoice in the fact that this ancient park scenery is being maintained as if the British, the ones who founded it, were still around…

~ The Powder ~

Premadasa stops on a country road by lots of small "shops".

According to European standards, these are better shacks where they sell anything you can imagine and anything a traveller might need or not need.

He disappears into a store, which is marked as a pharmacy by the large cross above the entrance. The letters proudly announce the blessing that modern medicine brings, which can be found anywhere, even here in the middle of the jungle.

Impatiently, I follow him into the shop and am instantly amazed at what I can see, the shelves are filled with tons of medicines from all kinds of places. It is only the interior of the pharmacy that gives away where the medicinal herbs and pills are located.

The shopkeeper is proud that his customers come from Europe. He shows us his range of products for fighting dog parasites, he even has dog dewormers from a large German pharmaceutical company on offer.

The prices are a joke. We pay a thousandth part of what we will later pay for the same products in Germany, even though these ones were additionally transported from Germany to Asia.

We look for a quiet spot by the side of the road. Gabriele managed to find a comb and a brush in a shop, now we are ready to brush and comb Tina's ruffled fur.

After that, we apply the powder again and again.

While several of us are pulling and tugging at our new fosterling, Tina joyfully chews on a bone that we took from the market.

She is very patient. She seems to know that we are trying to help her; I was very impressed by how trusting this small creature already was. She is not afraid of anyone or anything and she comes into our arms full of trust.

Ten minutes later the unbelievable happens: Hundreds, if not thousands of "corpses" fall off her small body. Parasites of all kinds, all sizes, lengths, and heights. Some almost invisible, others very large. They all lie dead on the smooth stone surface.

I would have never thought that there are as many different kinds of lice and ticks in the world, as I saw that day.

The powder was very effective, but obviously also highly toxic.

After Tina had received basic care, the next problem surfaced: Which barriers would we have to overcome in order to take this dog back home with us to Germany?!

I had no clue about which requirements she had to fulfil for transport. Was there a quarantine in Germany, did the Sri Lankan authorities have any restrictions in place for taking her out of the country?

I can think of another "shack business" story on the roadside:

We once stopped by the roadside during a trip, because there were several "bakery shack" that lured us in with tasty snacks.

The women go first, while we wait in the taxi, watching Tina. Tanja wants to buy some of the "baked goods" that look very tempting in the display window.

You have to put aside any concerns about the numerous flies that are always surrounding the open displays which aim to lure travellers in from the side of the road.

Both of them come back to the car smiling and hand us several delicious looking rolls and curly-shaped cakes, etc.

Suddenly Tanja screams loudly. „There are maggots in this!", she yells hysterically and shows us the curly-shaped roll that had something inside that was moving, it looked like maggots.

Without having the chance to take a closer look at this Corpus Delicti, to make sure that this hysterically expressed information is actually true, Tanja throws the pastry out the window pulling a disgusted face.

Immediately everyone follows suit, we are all disgusted, panicked, and appalled.

To this day, no one knows if there really was anything in these baked goods that was still alive, but as the name suggests something that was "baked" can't contain anything living.

~ At the Vet ~

The first step in dealing with the "problem" was a trip to the vet. I didn't have any expectations about the amount of medical care that was or was not available in this so called "Third World Country."

In Europe, it is commonly thought that such a country suffers from a medical crisis when it comes to medical care and doctors. This is by no means the case in Sri Lanka: There are doctors' surgeries almost on every corner and to my surprise, it wasn't a problem at all to find a vet. In fact, it was almost right around the corner of our lodging.

The first examination showed that she had received good first care when we got rid of the parasites. This gave Tina the chance to recover physically and performance-wise, because parasites weaken such a small body very much.

Our doctor was so pleased about us taking care and adopting an animal from the streets, that he offered to put an earlier date on the rabies vaccination.

The vaccination had to be carried out four weeks prior, in order to be granted entry into Germany. As our stay would end two weeks after we found Tina, this slight trick came in very handy for us.

We received an international vaccination card, which was even printed in Germany (we were so lucky, as the German customs officer asked us about it later; when I asked him what would have happened, had we not had this card, he said we would have not been allowed to take her with us!).

~ Bureaucracy ~

The locals recommended that in order to export Tina, we should obtain a permit from the "Department of the Ministry of Wildlife and Forest Conservation" in Colombo, the capital city of Sri Lanka.

Even though we were unsure if this was really necessary and since no one could give us any more information about it, we took a taxi to the capital city during the roaring heat and completed our mission under great hardships. We later found out that it was not necessary at all.

On that day we were sent from "Pontius to Pilate", until we finally reached the correct authority. We then received a meaningless piece of paper written in the Sinhala language and we could only trust that it was the document we were looking for.

We asked for directions on every street, until we finally found the right place[5], as there weren't any road maps we could have bought; if you ask 20 people, you will receive 20 different route descriptions! However, people are not trying to be rude, the locals often don't even know where specific offices are in the city they live in. But since they don't want to seem clueless in front of a foreigner, they try everything they can to help, often using "hands and feet".

In most cases, this leads to unavoidable confusion.

---

[5] Unfortunately, there weren't any navigation devices available yet.

So it happened that one office sent us to a different office and so on. All in all, it took us two days to obtain the correct document.

The same was true when we dealt with other authorities, i.e. the airline. It took us a total of four days in order to get everything sorted out. In Europe, you could have settled it all within a very short time by means of a few phone calls.

The people working in the airline's office sent us from one internal office to the next one. In the end, we circled back to the freight department, who in turn told us to go back to the main office.

Later we discovered a possible reason for this inconvenience: Sacrificing a handful of rupees would have opened doors and gates for us and since we were naive and didn't pay them anything, everything took longer. Looking back, however, I am proud that we didn't bribe anybody; it is still possible to do without in Asia. It only takes will power and lots of time and sacrifice.

I just had to assert myself, however, if I hadn't been able to speak English it would have become impossible to do.

The appropriate authorities of our airline were adamant that it was necessary to construct a special freight box for Tina. Apparently, the international aviation authority IATA required this.

This forced us to embark on an adventurous trip through the stuffy capital city of Sri Lanka, a city that should be called moloch, instead of city.

I had never before and nowhere else experienced such a blazing heat, reminiscent of a witch's cauldron, there was nothing comparable to this Asian metropolis. The fumes coming from the cars felt as if they were coming from an open fire, that emitted dark smoke.

I had passed through the city several times before on a motorbike. This turned out to be a terrible challenge. Within a few minutes, I was covered from head to toe with dust from the streets. I held my breath due to the terrible exhaust fumes from the men (and women??) in front of me. I almost suffocated in the stop and go traffic of this crazy city.

Another time I walked along a main road. The incredible heat was so strong on that day (actually it was like this every day), that I felt as though I was walking through a hot stone oven. My skin was burning, my breathing had stopped, it was simply unbearable. Never before and never again after that did I make such an extreme experience.

Back to our marathon tour through the city to ensure we could take Tina with us to Germany:

We were recommended a company that was working with wood. It was located on the outskirts of Colombo. With the help of our taxi driver, we managed to find the place.

The employees of this company were happy that we, being foreigners, asked them to build something. They constructed a beautiful wooden box in accordance with the requirements of the airline[6].

It weighed about 14 kilograms and was about the size of a suitcase, that people used to travel, right around the last turn of the century. The box was about 1 meter high

---

[6] See the drawing of that box on page 71.

and about 60 cm wide. There was enough room for our little puppy, who only weighed 2 kilograms, to move around during the 15-hour flight around half the world.

A crescent shaped door was also added in the upper area, that locked the box. The door was made from lattice and had hinges, which provided enough room to open and close it comfortably. If this box was built in Europe, it would have probably destroyed our travel budget completely. But in this country, they were happy to take DM[7] 50 (around 25 Euros today) and probably thought that they had made big business with us.

With the boot lid of "our" Morris-taxi half open, our taxi driver took the box from the capital city, Colombo, to the vicinity of the airport of Colombo. Our driver, Premadasa had a friend there who was happy to store the box at his home until we left. Due to its size, we couldn't keep the box in our hotel room.

The airline kept reassuring us that our dog would be safe and well protected in the freight space of the plane. They told us there was a set of stairs leading there from the passenger cabin, which the crew would use to provide the dog with food and water. We were excitedly and calmly looking forward to the day of our departure since we knew our darling would be safe and cared for.

---

[7] **DM** means "German (or Deutsch) Marks", the German currency from 1949-2002.

~ Tina's First Adventures ~

Tina was still small, so of course, there was no use trying to "house-train" her. She had never lived in an apartment or a house before, she didn't know about the conditions of living together with humans. Soon enough such a problem occurred on one of our tours, that we went on before going back to Germany.

We were travelling south of the capital city Colombo, to a place called Mount Lavinia. Due to frequent visits by Europeans, there were a large number of luxurious hotels there, right by the Indian Ocean. They reminded us of the "wonderful" old times of colonialism, as they were built in the beautiful colonial style.

We checked into a middle class hotel and even though we knew that dogs weren't allowed, we found a way to sneak Tina in.

As we were tired from the strains of the journey we didn't hesitate to use an old trick: Gabriele, one of our companions pretended to be my sick wife, by complaining loudly and dramatically in my arms. She was writhing with pain whilst sneaking past the reception with me.

Her bent over posture allowed us to hide our little darling in a bag by her stomach. This was how we smuggled Tina past the questioning glances of the hotel staff.

Tina was not used to being hidden, so she howled and whined. After all, she was a proud dog who was used to running through the world with her tail held high. Gabriele tried to cover up Tina's howling by lamenting loudly herself, which she did a great job of.

No one noticed our trick, at least for now. If only it wasn't for the fact that a puppy needs to use the bathroom for one or the other reason every few minutes.

We used a flokati carpet which had luckily been put in front of our bed, as a "kind of meadow".

When we had to leave the room, we weren't always able to take Tina with us, as the scene with the sick wife would have only been believable the first time. Whether we liked it or not, we had to leave Tina behind, for example when we went to eat in the dining hall.

This led to a staccato of lamenting and whining by the door of the hotel room. We realised that would not end well. The whole thing would be blown up by the next morning at the latest. And that was exactly what happened.

Early in the morning, the door of our room was opened by the hotel manager and several employees, without knocking first. They then kicked us out of the hotel without saying much. The manager was notified about the "wild dog" by the cleaning lady of our floor.

As we had only experienced devote friendliness and unwanted subservience of the locals up to this point, we were even more surprised how strict and determinately this hotel manager ran his business. All the talking and even numerous attempts at bribing him led to nothing, we had to leave the hotel.

Of course, our behaviour had not been okay, but the whole situation had overwhelmed us and what made it even worse was that we were young, braver and more daring than we would like today.

Since there were two days left until our departure, I remembered a local hotel right by the airport. From my experience of past trips it was a quiet and very tolerant place.

We were almost on our own there and there was enough room so that we could officially check-in together with our darling. It was Tina's first official stay at a hotel. A good start for a new life in a civilised world full of new wonders...

~ Visiting the Zoo ~

While Manuel and I still had a few things to do regarding Tina, two of our companions, Tanja and Gabriele went on a trip to the zoo in Colombo.

Not only did this zoo have plenty of rare animals, it was especially interesting when it came to "studying" the locals in this country.

Lots of children, entire school classes, and other large crowds came to the zoo to admire the large variety of animals in Sri Lanka in person. This kind of trip to the zoo was not just any trip. No, it was an event that you would only participate in once or twice a year.

In order to celebrate this special day, the people of Sri Lanka put on their best costumes, the finest and most colourful clothes; often you can see the boys wearing symbols, that are also very special on their own: Western clothing like jeans or nylon shirts with corresponding well known brand logos.

People don't come to visit the zoo for one or two hours only, they will spend the entire day there, taking the time for an extensive picnic or rice and curry meal, which was wrapped in paper, brought along to the trip and eaten on top of the first patch of grass they can find. Sometimes they share some with the animals.

However, some of the animal cages are less comfortable than that. Lions are left with very small kennels, in which they walk back and forth, as this is the only movement they are able to do (described as hospitalism[8]).

Monkeys are also not allowed to sit on rocks in open-air enclosures, as you would see in European zoos; they too, spend their existence in small individual cages. It is a shame that the awareness, which has long since been realised in European zoos, has not been realised here yet. Namely that zoos should no longer be like prisons.

In this way visiting the zoo is an interesting experience for us, because we watch the behaviour of the other visitors. The diversity, grace, happiness, and hunger for knowledge of these wonderful people is unique and contagious.

However, the animals and the situation they are in is very unfortunate.

This incident surprised me greatly. Usually the followers of Buddhism have great respect for all creatures. Especially due to the Buddhist belief, that one could be reincarnated as an animal, either in his or her previous or next life.

---

[8] **"Hospitalism** (or *anaclitic depression* in its sublethal form) was a pediatric diagnosis used in the 1930s to describe infants who wasted away while in hospital. The symptoms could include retarded physical development, and disruption of perceptual-motor skills and language. It is now understood that this wasting disease was mostly caused by a lack of social contact between the infant and its caregivers." Internet quoting: URL. https://en.wikipedia.org/wiki/Hospitalism. Status: Nov., 12th, 2020.

As it is the case with many religions in the world, belief and reality are often far from being the same.

It was one of the many contradictions that we noticed again and again in the many years of visiting Sri Lanka in particular. This got us thinking and shivering.

~ Evil Intentions ~

Despite of these negative impressions, Tanja and Gabriele returned from their trip enthusiastically and told us the following story:

When they sat down to have some tea at a café in the zoo, a well-dressed man approached them and started a conversation with the both of them.

At first, he asked if they had any cigarettes, he then very skilfully made up a story that the two adult women fell for innocently.

Through a clever trick, the elegant man quickly found out that the two ladies were from Germany and would return home in two days.

He quickly pretended to be the co-pilot of their flight, who was employed by the Sri Lanka airline.

The women were amazed as they thought they would do a favour to Manuel and me if they told this man the whole story about Tina.

Our plan to take home a dog would not cause any problems, the man said. He offered to help us out, so that we could spare ourselves all the inconvenience that comes with the paperwork of travelling with a dog.

He offered to "sneak us past" customs and other checkpoints. The entire endeavour was obviously entirely selfless because he liked Germans very much and appreciated German passengers on his flights in particular. However, he had to go and prepare some things and it wouldn't hurt if we paid him a small fee upfront, just in case.

Neither of the women was suspicious at any point. As they would later tell us, the only thing that seemed strange to Tanja was that this elegant man kept taking her cigarettes during the conversation, even though he didn't ask for permission again.

I think her inner voice was a bit more attentive in this area, but it was too late. They readily emptied their wallets and gathered an incredible amount of money, for Sri Lanka standards at least.

When Manuel heard that the ladies had also revealed our private address in Germany as well as our current hotel address to the man, so that he could make sure that all his efforts would be safe, Manuel's patience came to an end. He started panicking and urged us to change hotels immediately, so that we wouldn't be robbed by any other friendly helpers at night or when we were out.

Of course, I was also shocked by the naivety of the two women, but also by the cleverness of that man.

I was seriously worried about the fact that he knew our address in Germany. I'm sure it would have been very easy for the man to tell his friends in Germany about the vacant apartment, which they could have plundered in peace.

However, we were very relieved when we returned to Germany and found out all our belongings were still in the same place.

~ Sigiriya ~

Sigiriya (which means lion's rock) is a small and very old settlement, surrounded by a water ditch and situated around a unique and unusual rock.

The monolithic rock looks as if it was planted by a giant in the middle of the jungle plain. It became famous when UNESCO declared it a world heritage site in 1982. Ever since then thousands of visitors come to admire it regularly.

The area around this "little" gem is adorned with beautifully renovated gardens, remnants of water fountains, pavilions, and former monastery sites[9].

A short distance from the rock there is a fantastic hotel, which carefully blends into the surrounding landscape. The hotel offers a large outdoor swimming pool and small table arrangements on the grounds around it.

If you sit there in the evening while having dinner, you get to witness a picturesque view of the rock and its surrounding jungle. It is the most romantic way to dine.

---

[9] See also source on the Internet: URL. https://en.wikipedia.org/wiki/Sigiriya.html. Keyword Sigiriya. Status: Oct. 26th 2020.

I have often travelled to this wonderful relaxation zone in the middle of the jungle and spent a few days there, in order to recover from the stress of the road traffic.

I often used a motorbike for my trips. Riding a motorbike in Sri Lanka is not just an adventure, it is also a lot of work. A drive over old road paths with lots of holes in them is very stressful for your back and your whole body.

Bumps, dust, dirt, and loud noise as well as the unforgettable stressful traffic create the need for the driver to take a break every half an hour, in order to grant the body some relief.

In addition to that, you have to get used to driving on the left side, which usually becomes a habit quite quickly.

Right before left also applies when driving on the left side. But you should make sure that the motorbike (and any other vehicle) is fitted with a horn. Without it, you are doomed.

Traffic rules are usually only observed rudimentary. Honking plays an important role, in order to let others know: 'Here I come and make sure not to get in my way!'.

The opposite person thinks the same thing, so oftentimes the only thing you can do is hope that the smarter one of the two gives in.

Despite these conditions, the traffic runs quite smoothly and seems to regulate itself, similar to a swarm of bees.

Of course, there are plenty of severe accidents around here. But there is still a relatively low number in proportion. India takes first place with 150,785 deaths. One thing is for sure, it definitely takes getting used to for a Central European (and others) and it is still very dangerous in some situations.[10]

If you feel fit enough you should enjoy this experience. If you've gone for a ride once, you'll agree that it is absolutely incredible. It is like another rush that you can't get anywhere else.

Apart from the physical strain, it is a great way to get to know the country and its people.

In 1981, we were driving through villages and the countryside on motor scooters. Whenever we stopped in a village or a settlement to have a drink or a snack, large groups of people, mostly children, gathered to watch us eat a banana, as if they had never seen white people eat.

At first, this made us quite uncomfortable, but we quickly got used to it. Especially because we often had funny little conversations and talking to these curious people was good for us.

---

[10] The number of road deaths per 100,000 inhabitants amounts to 3,003 deaths in Sri Lanka (official estimate), which ranks 36th in the world, Germany ranks 33rd with 3,206 deaths. Information by Road Safety Report 2018 of the World Health Organisation, valid for 2016. Internet quoting:
URL. https://de.wikipedia.org/wiki/Liste_der_Länder_nach_Verkehrstoten.html.
Status: Oct. 17th 2020. Translated from German by Angelika Hinchcliffe, UK.

Nevertheless, it was unfamiliar and sometimes scary. Because there were literally hundreds of people standing by the roadside.

Back then I wrote down my memories of a ride on the motorbike, in order to capture the feelings that rose up in me:

"Despite the wind and only wearing shorts and a t-shirt, the seat of the motorbike is very hot.

It felt like driving through a hot oven, I drive on worn out asphalt with a grooved structure that could force a motorbike into the sand and dust on the roadside.

Here, in the centre of the Sri Lanka highlands, there is almost no one crossing my path. At most, a few locals are standing by the roadside now and again. They are surprised that brave tourists ride through the countryside.

Despite driving on the left side and the sometimes dangerous behaviour of the Sri Lanka people, I am having a lot of fun driving hundreds of kilometres through the jungle landscape, without any traffic lights, traffic jams, or other reasons to stop.

Nevertheless, I have to stop every half an hour or else my back and posterior wouldn't be able to stand the strain.

Without a horn, my dangerous adventure tour would be an absolute nightmare with no guarantee of making it out unscathed.

People, as well as animals only react to the warning sound of the horn. Not even the sound of the engine would be able to startle a dog that is sleeping in the middle of the road. They often lie in the middle of the up North leading country roads and sleep soundly.

It is only due to the sound of the horn that they wake up and stumble away from the road.

They often pull a face that suggests: ,Another one of these annoying human vehicles that won't let me take my five hour nap in peace!'

And: ,Another one of these white humans sitting on it!'

Shortly after they had this thought and the vehicle had left, they went back to the exact same spot on the street in order to continue their well deserved nap.

Out of nowhere, a roadblock appears in the middle of the country road. At first, it is not clear to me what the point of this barrier was.

Suddenly I see a small guardhouse on the roadside. Out comes a soldier who seems to realise I am a tourist, not a terrorist after I lift the visor on my helmet. He gives me a wave and tells me to drive on, without checking me."

Back then you would often see these checkpoints along the country roads in the North, as I would later find out. They were supposed to stop the delivery of arms from Tamil guerrillas to renegade Tamil strongholds in the North (as part of the fight for an independent Tamil "Elam").

There was a rumour that the guerrillas used tourists as human shields or even abducted them.

I never made any experiences with that, I was always able to travel the land undisturbed and unchecked.

~ Departure ~

The day of departure came closer and closer and I became more and more nervous. Despite the promises from the airline, I mostly worried about whether Tina would survive the flight unscathed.

Of course, I took precautions and had acquired a Valium pill. But just the thought that Tina had to spend 15 hours in a box seemed "inhumane" to me, to say the least.

Then finally the day of all days arrived.

The giant constructed box slowly disappeared into the belly of the machine.

We were given permission to enter the airfield and put Tina's box onto the conveyer belt ourselves. My heart was racing and everything inside of me shrank into an incredibly tight ball. At least it wouldn't take too long until I could be with her. We were promised that we could do that anytime.

~ Our Flight Home ~

I waited impatiently for the first stopover three hours later.

During the flight, we were told that it wasn't possible to enter the freight area via the promised set of stairs. The first shock!

The crew swapped over during the overlay. No one in this new crew knew anything about the promises the airline and the first crew had made to us! Access was not possible. But they would try to organise something during the second layover.

The second stop came around after an agonisingly long time of waiting, but again accessing the area was not possible. I was furious.

It was only after lengthy and stressful discussions that I was allowed to enter the airfield and the cargo ramp, while the engines were running and roaring.

A moving staircase was attached to the plane and the box with our dog inside was brought onto the runway. I then had a few minutes to put some food and a bowl full of water into her box.

This was the exact reason for this stressful situation: Since we were promised that we could have access to her during the flight, we didn't give her any food or water in her box. We worried that she would be so frantic during the flight that she would become very thirsty and that this could harm her! This was the winning argument that helped us get access.

The encounter on the runway was like hell. I saw how our little one was eaten up by fear of the loud engine noise and she didn't understand what was happening as she sat in the oversized box (at least she had enough room!).

Tina screamed as she would in the future whenever she was scared or panicked and wanted to warn us. It was heartbreaking, disturbing! It was the worst moment of my life.

I left her again, crying, not looking back, as the box was put back in storage, as the door of the cargo space was closed. I climbed back into the belly of this terrible vehicle…

Manuel asked what it was like, I stayed silent and cried on the inside. He understood and was also silent. Deep darkness covered my soul.

~ After Landing ~

Arriving in Schiphol, Netherlands was the most exciting moment ever.

We were told that the dog would arrive through a container elevator at the farthest corner of the airport hall. Huge gates towered in front of us. We were shaking with excitement. It seemed to take ages.

Then finally the impossible happened: the gates open-end and Tina's huge box was in it all by itself. A tiny being greeted us with a joyful howling and strong tail wagging. We quickly forgot about all the stress of the last few hours, what felt like days, or even years. Tina was alright!

An incredible scene unfolded! We were overjoyed. This little creature had exhibited so much bravery, she seemed to be better than us! We released her from her prison cell and just left the box in some corner, as we were instructed by the airline employee. It was a pity because it was beautifully constructed and had made it possible for Tina to join us on our journey home. Nevertheless, we didn't miss it. We had Tina after all and that was the best thing in that moment.

~ A Long Life ~

Tina would be getting 17 years and five days old.

Of course, we didn't know her exact birthday, but we gave her a fake one. According to this, she was born on January 7th, 1990 and she died on January, 12st ,2007.

She was a great dog, smart and intelligent.

Never once in 13 years did she fight with her "sister" Mickey who would join the family later; never, not even once.

She lived a long, fulfilled life. Full of joy and happiness. She changed everything, my whole life became different; richer, happier, more fulfilled.

~ Epilogue ~

Tina and I are still deeply connected, she has become a part of my soul. She watched over me during all the bad times that were yet to come. She never complained, was never angry, always gentle, and loving.

I still love her as I did on the very first day in 1990 and it will always be like that. We are connected for all eternity. Her ashes are always with me; her urn is never far, in every moment. Tina really was

my best friend

and she will always be my best friend.

Tina's transport box.
Drawn by Craig, Manchester, UK